From The Heart of A Worshiper:

A Book of Love Letters

Written
by

ANDREA R.W. VAUGHAN

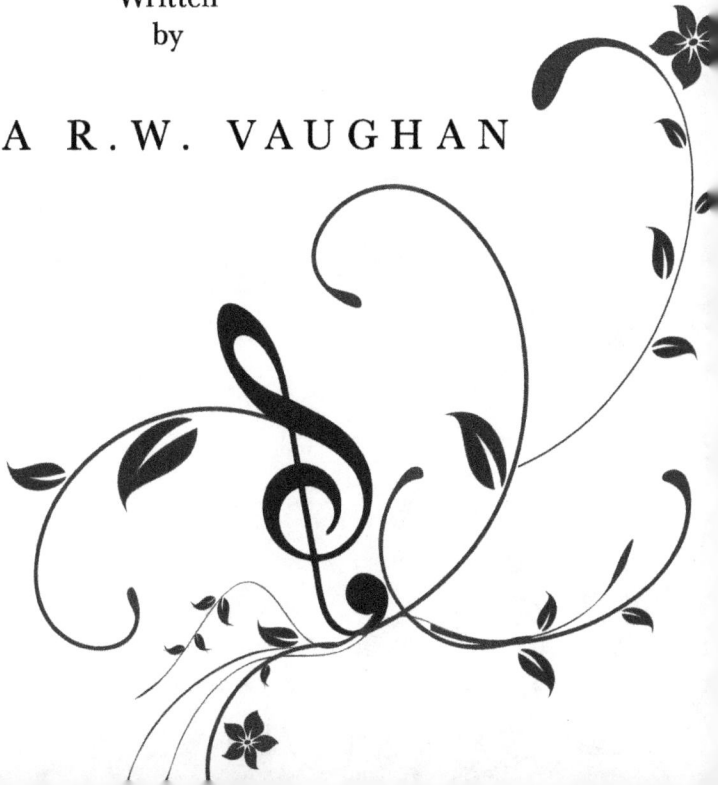

Contribution by Kiyanni Bryan, Write It Out Publishing LLC
in the United States of America.

Cover Illustrator: Maurice Rogers
Intext Illustrator: Jason Josiah
Editor: Tamira K. Butler-Likely

ISBN: 978-1-7358024-9-7(PaperBack)
First Printing, 2021

Andrea R.W. Vaughan
Chesapeake, Virginia

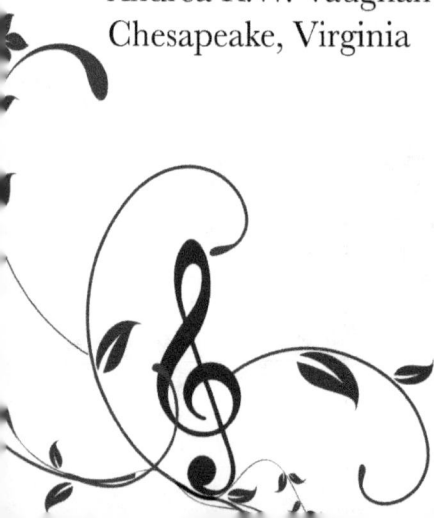

Dedication

I dedicate this book to my Lord and Savior Jesus Christ. Without the gifts and talents that he has given me, this book would not have come into fruition. I also dedicate this book to my husband, Paul Vaughan, Sr., who believes in me and pushes me to be the best that I can be, and who loves me unconditionally. Lastly, I dedicate this book to my family and friends who believed in me even when I didn't. I Love You.

Book Foreword

I'm proud of my wife. She worked long and hard, every word in this book comes from her heart and spirit. This is just the first of many to come, and I'm excited to see it manifest.

- Mr. Paul Vaughan, Sr., Husband

In reading this book written by Andrea R. Vaughan, there will be an awakening of the true love of God and the beauty of his word towards us. Through Mrs. Vaughan's grasp of "poetic scriptural verse," I hope and pray that you, the readers, will experience God, the master poet of the universe, in a whole new and different way.

- Prophet Bruce and Prophetess Renee Payton

Prologue:

Psalm 42:1-2 (NKJV) As the deer pants for the water brooks, so pants my soul for you, O God. My soul thirsts for God, for the living God. When shall I come and appear before God?

Table of Contents

Introduction:

The book you are about to read is from a person who wants everyone to experience God on a personal level, on a daily basis, in a new and refreshing way. The love that one has in expressing the deep feelings, gratitude, and thanksgiving will be displayed in this beautiful and awesome art, which is poetry. It goes from one extreme of thought to another leap of faith, acknowledgement, and worship. This is a collection of poems that you have probably never seen or heard. The takeaway after one reads and ponders every word, the author hopes, is that you yourself will go one step further in knowing Jesus this way.

From The Heart of A Worshiper:

A Book of Love Letters

Written
by

ANDREA R.W. VAUGHAN

ANDREA R.W. VAUGHAN

I WISH

I wish I could tell you,
What I've been thinking,
The thoughts that've been traveling,
Through my mind.

I wish I could say,
What I really want to,
To express the feelings,
In my heart.

I wish I could convey,
My true emotions,
Things I can't speak on,
True inner expressions.

So much I see,
So much I don't say,
But that's okay,
It will all come out sooner or later,
But for now...
I wish.

ONE OF MANY

I am one of many,
That have faced trials,
Gone through hard times,
And still can smile—after a while.

I am one of many,
That have cried tears of anger,
Felt hopeless,
But still kept going.

I am one of many,
That wonder why,
Want to know how,
To make things right.

I thank God,
For keeping me,
For building me up,
To be, one of many.

YOUR SUSTAINING POWER

The power to love,
To reach out,
The power to pray,
While in deep depression,
The power to stand,
When you feel like falling down,
The power to rise,
Above...

The power to hold on,
To my faith in you, God,
The power to decree and declare,
What you have spoken,
The power to keep holding on,
When I wanna let go,
And give up...

• • • •

I acknowledge my wrong,
I have the power to confess,
I have the power to change,
I have the power to forgive,
God, you gave me the power.

As long as I got you, God,
I have all I need,
As long as I got you, Jesus,
I can make it through,
As long as I got you, Savior,
I can't lose.

Do one thing for me, Lord,
Don't take away your Sustaining
Power!

REMEMBER

I often think about,
How it used to be,
When I was growing up,
Fancy and Free.

Playing outside,
Blowing bubbles, playing hopscotch,
Going to the ice cream truck,
Dad buying neighborhood kids ice cream too.

Riding my bike,
Filling the little pool with water,
Putting on my bathing suit, me and my friends,
Splashing in the water.

Playing kickball, dodge ball,
1, 2, 3 red light, trying to double dutch,
And frisbee—I loved frisbee!!!
I was a pro, of course, my dad taught me.

Walking up to my house after school,
Getting halfway there and smelling fried chicken,
My friends asking if they could eat at my house,
Sleepovers were the best.

• • • •

• • • •

Getting in serious trouble with Mom and Dad,
For doing stupid stuff,
I'm remembering times of growth and youth,
The good ole days, as they say.

Times change, people change,
Gotta grow up, experience life,
Will have some great times,
And then deal with some real difficult days,
Times when you laugh and times when you cry,
Sometimes the crying lasts a little long, but...
The sun comes up and you are back to life.

It's experiences that bring you to right now,
All the ingredients of what makes your life worth
living.
Can't forget them, have no regrets just
—remember.

I'M READY

To experience a new way,
Experience a new day,
New life, New love,
I'm Ready.

To step out on faith,
To walk in my new experience,
To speak with passion,
Oh yes, I'm Ready.

To hold on to God,
Like never before,
To trust without fail,
I'm Ready.

To be what he says I am,
To have what he said I could,
To open up my heart to him,
Lord, I'm Ready.

MY SONG

My song is just that,
From every piece of me,
From deep in my heart,
A song of love.

I'm ready to release,
To give it my all,
My heart and soul,
A song of praise.

Excited, Anxious,
Ready to come out,
Adoration and joy,
A song of happiness.

I wanna show you my passion,
I need to tell you my gratitude,
I have to give you my all,
Father, here is my song.

LET IT GO!

I refuse to worry,
It don't please you,
I've got to trust you,
And release it to you.

Let you handle it,
Let you have it,
Let you settle it,
Once and for all.

Worry takes sleep away,
Worry takes joy away,
Worry takes smiles away,
It robs you of peace.

Got to overcome worry,
Stop it completely,
Let God have all,
Worry must cease!

YOUR PRESENCE

The peace that you bring,
The song that you sing,
The calm to my storm,
The right to my wrong.

Joy comes in abundance,
Rest comes oh so sweetly,
Your voice is softly received,
Your love is strong for me.

Refreshing for my soul,
Spirit rejuvenated,
Awareness heightened,
My strength is being renewed!

Precious Holy Spirit,
You are my refuge,
I'm nothing without you,
Thank you God for your awesome pres-
ence!

YOU

Jesus, you are my heart,
I look to you for my help,
You are my Lord, I depend on you,
I lean on your every word.

I trust you more and more,
For you are my hope,
When all else fails,
You stand with authority.

Lord, you are glorious,
You are Holy,
I find my healing in you,
You are all I need.

Learning more and more,
To rely on you, my King,
I will always look to you,
My Everything.

PAUL

My only one,
My only love,
Loves me for real,
From the heart.

Been there for me,
Always in my corner,
Defends me at all cost,
Shields and protects me.

We were friends first,
Talking and laughing,
Sharing with one another,
Our goals and dreams.

Been together for some time,
Still going strong,
Thank God for him every day,
My Paul.

THAT PLACE

There is a place of peace,
That every believer must reach,
It's a place of serenity,
A place of ultimate surrender.

Pour out your heart,
Your mind, every thought you can
release,
Your doubts, your fears,
Your worries he will cease.

Gotta get to that place in God,
Broken hearts will be healed,
Broken spirits will be healed,
Oh how I love that place of prayer.

I want to stay in this secret place,
A place of protection,
A place of stability,
Thank you God for being that place.

So when you're in trouble—run to
that place,
When you are seeking refuge—run to
that place,
When you can't see your way—run,
run to God's place,
His arms are wide open,
Get to that place!

WHEN YOU LEAST EXPECT IT

Someone shows you love,
Someone shows you gratitude,
Someone gives you a smile,
Someone says hello...

When you least expect it

There are flowers at your door,
Someone treats you to dinner,
Someone gives you a card,
Someone says thank you...

When you least expect it

You are filled with peace,
Peace you don't understand,
You are filled with joy,
It's a great feeling,
The thoughtfulness of others,
The gratitude of people,
The love of all...when you least
expect it.

LORD, YOU ARE MY SOURCE

Source of power
Strength
Wisdom
Courage...

Of understanding
Of knowledge
Of grace
Of mercy...

Of companionship
Of friendship
Of excellence
Of healing...

Of peace
Of tranquility
Of joy...

Lord, You Are My Source.

YOU ARE WITH ME

In my sad times
In my good times
In trials and tests
You are with me.

Times of anguish
Times of pain
Times of grief
You are with me.

When I'm down
When I'm alone
When I can't see my way
Your light is with me.

All my ups
All my downs
All my days
Lord, you have been with me.
Thank you.

MOVE

Where I am going
No one knows but God
My footsteps are ordered
And I'm willing to follow him.

There's a lot that I'm not sure of
A lot I'm reluctant about
Much that I'm cautious of
But, I'll keep walking your way,
Lord.

I'm holding on to faith
No matter how shaky I am
Lord, teach me to trust you more
No more hesitation.

Lord, thank you for giving me
The power to stand
The strength to hold on
I submit, I surrender.

GOD, ONLY YOU

I'm a mess
But only you can clean me up,

I'm lost
But only you can get me right,

I'm in trouble
But only you can rescue me,

I'm in need
But only you can supply,

I'm bound
But only you can set me free,

I'm scared
But only you can remove fear and make
me bold,

I've sinned
But only you can forgive me,
I trust you, God, ONLY YOU!

REACHING

I'm reaching out for you
No matter what I have to do
My sights are on you
I'm focused...

I need you to fix me
Can't fix myself
Tried to and failed
I'm desperate...

Need answers from you
Can't go to no one else
Don't want to
I just want you, Lord...

I know you hear me
I know you'll answer
I will obey you
I'll keep on reaching.

TOO MUCH

Too much pain and sorrow,
Too much worrying about tomorrow,
Too much friction between the races,
Too many tear-stained faces...

When will the hurt and agony end,
When are we going to smile again,
When are we going to know the truth,
Too many lies, too much deceit...

The love of many has grown cold,
Wonder if there was love there at all,
All of the turmoil has to cease,
Waiting for a moment of a release of
peace...

Jesus, we need you to wipe the tears,
Console us and give us strength,
Speak the peace we need to hear,
Change sorrow into joy...because
Lord, it's just been TOO MUCH!

THANK YOU FOR THAT

For your peace
I thank you for that
For never leaving me
I thank you for that
For covering me
I thank you for that
For love that never ceases
I thank you for that.

For joy to the full
I thank you for that
For my mind being stable
I thank you for that
For justifying me
I thank you for that
For sanctification
I thank you for that.

For protecting me
For your shield
For your presence
For your care
Father God, I thank you for that.

No one could do what you do
No one would ever try
For everything you are
I will forever thank you for that.

SO MUCH

So much has been done
So much has been said
So much has been seen
So much has been heard.

So many have been hurt
So many have been wounded
So many have been used
So many have been abused.

There are people who doubt
There are people who laugh
People who stand in amazement
People who don't know why.

So, what is the answer?
What is the next step?
What is the only solution?
What is the strategic plan...

PRAYER!